Gratitude Journal

- -

Journal five minutes a day to develop gratitude,
mindfulness and productivity

90 Days of daily practice, spending five minutes to cultivate happiness

My Goals/Thoughts/Plans for the next 90 days

Make Gratitude your new habit

As you practice your new habit each day,

Celebrate your progress and check off each day of your efforts!

Week 1	1	2	3	4	5	6	7	1
Week 2	8	9	10	11	12	13	14	2
Week 3	15	16	17	18	19	20	21	3
Week 4	22	23	24	25	26	27	28	4
Week 5	29	30	31	32	33	34	35	5
Week 6	36	37	38	39	40	41	42	6
Week 7	43	44	45	46	47	48	49	7
Week 8	50	51	52	53	54	55	56	8
Week 9	57	58	59	60	61	62	63	9
Week 10	64	65	66	67	68	69	70	10
Week 11	71	72	73	74	75	76	77	11
Week 12	78	79	80	81	82	83	84	12
Week 13	85	86	87	88	89	90		13

My monthly plans:

"You must be the change you wish to see in the world."
– Mahatma Gandhi

Goals I envision:

_____

_____

_____

Improvements I seek:

_____

_____

_____

Notes:

_____

_____

_____

Today, I am grateful for:

_____

_____

_____

How will I make today awesome?

_____

_____

Positive affirmations:

_____

_____

*"We are what we repeatedly do.
Excellence, then, is not an act, but a habit."
– Aristotle*

Today's amazing moments:

_____

_____

_____

How could I have made this day even better?

_____

_____

_____

Goals/Plans for Tomorrow: I am feeling:

_____   ☺ 😐 ☹

Date: ____/ ____/ _____

Today, I am grateful for:

_____

_____

_____

How will I make today awesome?

_____

_____

_____

Positive affirmations:

_____

_____

_____

*"Learn to be thankful for what you already have,
while you pursue all that you want."*
– Jim Rohn

Today's amazing moments:

_____

_____

_____

How could I have made this day even better?

_____

_____

_____

Goals/Plans for Tomorrow: I am feeling:

_____   😊   😐   🙁

_____

Date: ____/ ____/ _____

Today, I am grateful for:

_____

_____

_____

How will I make today awesome?

_____

_____

_____

Positive affirmations:

_____

_____

_____

"Each morning we are born again.
What we do today is what matters most."
– Buddha

Today's amazing moments:

_____

_____

_____

How could I have made this day even better?

_____

_____

_____

Goals/Plans for Tomorrow: I am feeling:

_____

_____   😊 😐 ☹️

Date: ____ / ____ / _____

Today, I am grateful for:

_____
_____
_____

How will I make today awesome?

_____
_____
_____

Positive affirmations:

_____
_____
_____

"Make each day your masterpiece."
– John Wooden

Today's amazing moments:

_____
_____
_____

How could I have made this day even better?

_____
_____
_____

Goals/Plans for Tomorrow: I am feeling:

_____
_____   ☺ ☺ ☹

Date: _____ / _____ / _____

Today, I am grateful for:

_____

_____

_____

How will I make today awesome?

_____

_____

_____

Positive affirmations:

_____

_____

_____

"Give every day the chance to become
the most beautiful day of your life."
– Mark Twain

Today's amazing moments:

_____

_____

_____

How could I have made this day even better?

_____

_____

_____

Goals/Plans for Tomorrow: I am feeling:

_____   ☺   😐   ☹

_____

Date: ____/ ____/ _____

Today, I am grateful for:

_____

_____

_____

How will I make today awesome?

_____

_____

_____

Positive affirmations:

_____

_____

_____

"Action is the foundational key to all success."
– Pablo Picasso

Today's amazing moments:

_____

_____

_____

How could I have made this day even better?

_____

_____

_____

Goals/Plans for Tomorrow: I am feeling:

_____

_____   :) :| :(

Date: _____ / _____ / _____

Today, I am grateful for:

_____

_____

_____

How will I make today awesome?

_____

_____

Positive affirmations:

_____

_____

"Someday is not a day of the week."
– Denise Brennan-Nelson

Today's amazing moments:

_____

_____

How could I have made this day even better?

_____

_____

Goals/Plans for Tomorrow: I am feeling:

_____
                                              ☺ 😐 ☹
_____

Date: ____ / ____ / _____

Today, I am grateful for:

_____

_____

_____

How will I make today awesome?

_____

_____

Positive affirmations:

_____

_____

_____

"Success occurs when opportunity meets preparation."
– Zig Ziglar

Today's amazing moments:

_____

_____

_____

How could I have made this day even better?

_____

_____

_____

Goals/Plans for Tomorrow: I am feeling:

_____

_____   😊 😐 ☹️

Date: _____/ _____/ _____

Today, I am grateful for:

_____

_____

_____

How will I make today awesome?

_____

_____

_____

Positive affirmations:

_____

_____

_____

"The best dreams happen when you're awake."
– Cherie Gilderbloom

Today's amazing moments:

_____

_____

_____

How could I have made this day even better?

_____

_____

_____

Goals/Plans for Tomorrow: I am feeling:

_____

_____   ☺ 😐 ☹

13

Date: _____ / _____ / _____

Today, I am grateful for:

_____

_____

_____

How will I make today awesome?

_____

_____

_____

Positive affirmations:

_____

_____

_____

"Don't count the days, make the days count."
– Muhammad Ali

Today's amazing moments:

_____

_____

_____

How could I have made this day even better?

_____

_____

_____

Goals/Plans for Tomorrow: I am feeling:

_____

_____   😊   😐   ☹️

Date: _____/ _____/ _____

Today, I am grateful for:

_____

_____

_____

How will I make today awesome?

_____

_____

_____

Positive affirmations:

_____

_____

_____

*"The difference between ordinary and
extraordinary is that little extra."*
– Jimmy Johnson

Today's amazing moments:

_____

_____

_____

How could I have made this day even better?

_____

_____

_____

Goals/Plans for Tomorrow: I am feeling:

_____

_____   ☺   ☺   ☹

Date: _____ / _____ / _____

Today, I am grateful for:

_____

_____

_____

How will I make today awesome?

_____

_____

Positive affirmations:

_____

_____

_____

"It's time to start living the life you've imagined
– Henry James

Today's amazing moments:

_____

_____

_____

How could I have made this day even better?

_____

_____

_____

Goals/Plans for Tomorrow: I am feeling:

_____   😊 😐 ☹️

Date: ____/ ____/ _____

Today, I am grateful for:

_____

_____

_____

How will I make today awesome?

_____

_____

_____

Positive affirmations:

_____

_____

_____

"If there is no struggle, there is no progress."
– Frederick Douglass

Today's amazing moments:

_____

_____

_____

How could I have made this day even better?

_____

_____

_____

Goals/Plans for Tomorrow: I am feeling:

_____

_____   ☺ 😐 ☹

17

Date: ____/ ____/ _____

Today, I am grateful for:

_____

_____

_____

How will I make today awesome?

_____

_____

_____

Positive affirmations:

_____

_____

_____

"The more I want to get something done,
the less I call it work."
– Richard Bach

Today's amazing moments:

_____

_____

_____

How could I have made this day even better?

_____

_____

_____

Goals/Plans for Tomorrow: I am feeling:

_____

_____

Date: _____/ _____/ _____

Today, I am grateful for:

_____
_____
_____

How will I make today awesome?

_____
_____
_____

Positive affirmations:

_____
_____
_____

"My future starts when I wake up every morning."
– Miles Davis

Today's amazing moments:

_____
_____
_____

How could I have made this day even better?

_____
_____
_____

Goals/Plans for Tomorrow: I am feeling:

_____   ☺ 😐 ☹
_____

Today, I am grateful for:

_____

_____

_____

How will I make today awesome?

_____

_____

_____

Positive affirmations:

_____

_____

_____

"A year from now you may wish you had started today."
– Karen Lamb

Today's amazing moments:

_____

_____

_____

How could I have made this day even better?

_____

_____

_____

Goals/Plans for Tomorrow: I am feeling:

_____

_____

Date: ____/ ____/ _____

Today, I am grateful for:

_____

_____

_____

How will I make today awesome?

_____

_____

_____

Positive affirmations:

_____

_____

_____

"Be willing to be a beginner every single morning."
– Meister Eckhart

Today's amazing moments:

_____

_____

_____

How could I have made this day even better?

_____

_____

_____

Goals/Plans for Tomorrow: I am feeling:

_____

_____   ☺   😐   ☹

Today, I am grateful for:

How will I make today awesome?

Positive affirmations:

"If you aren't going all the way, why go at all?"
-- Joe Namath

Today's amazing moments:

How could I have made this day even better?

Goals/Plans for Tomorrow: I am feeling:

☺ 😐 ☹

Date: ____ / ____ / _____

Today, I am grateful for:

_____

_____

_____

How will I make today awesome?

_____

_____

Positive affirmations:

_____

_____

_____

*"Become the person who would
attract the results you seek."*
– Jim Cathcart

Today's amazing moments:

_____

_____

_____

How could I have made this day even better?

_____

_____

_____

Goals/Plans for Tomorrow: I am feeling:

_____   😊 😐 😟

_____

Today, I am grateful for:

_____

_____

_____

How will I make today awesome?

_____

_____

_____

Positive affirmations:

_____

_____

_____

"Act as if what you do makes a difference.
It does."
– William James

Today's amazing moments:

_____

_____

_____

How could I have made this day even better?

_____

_____

_____

Goals/Plans for Tomorrow: I am feeling:

_____

_____   😊 😐 ☹️

Date: ____/ ____/ _____

Today, I am grateful for:

_____

_____

_____

How will I make today awesome?

_____

_____

Positive affirmations:

_____

_____

_____

"Begin by always expecting good things to happen."
– Tom Hopkins

Today's amazing moments:

_____

_____

_____

How could I have made this day even better?

_____

_____

_____

Goals/Plans for Tomorrow: I am feeling:

_____   ☺ 😐 ☹

_____

Today, I am grateful for:

_____

_____

_____

How will I make today awesome?

_____

_____

Positive affirmations:

_____

_____

"Don't be pushed by your problems.
Be led by your dreams."
– Ralph Waldo Emerson

Today's amazing moments:

_____

_____

_____

How could I have made this day even better?

_____

_____

_____

Goals/Plans for Tomorrow: I am feeling:

_____

_____   ☺ ☻ ☹

Date: ____/ ____/ _____

Today, I am grateful for:

_____

_____

_____

How will I make today awesome?

_____

_____

_____

Positive affirmations:

_____

_____

_____

""Don't watch the clock; do what it does.
Keep going."
– Sam Levenson

Today's amazing moments:

_____

_____

_____

How could I have made this day even better?

_____

_____

_____

Goals/Plans for Tomorrow: I am feeling:

_____

_____   ☺ 😐 ☹

Today, I am grateful for:

_____

_____

_____

How will I make today awesome?

_____

_____

Positive affirmations:

_____

_____

_____

"The harder I work, the luckier I get."
-- Gary Player

Today's amazing moments:

_____

_____

_____

How could I have made this day even better?

_____

_____

_____

Goals/Plans for Tomorrow: I am feeling:

_____   😊   😐   🙁

Date: _____/ _____/ _____

Today, I am grateful for:

_____

_____

_____

How will I make today awesome?

_____

_____

Positive affirmations:

_____

_____

_____

"You are what you do, not what you say you'll do."
– C.G. Jung

Today's amazing moments:

_____

_____

_____

How could I have made this day even better?

_____

_____

_____

Goals/Plans for Tomorrow: I am feeling:

_____

_____   ☺ 😐 ☹

Date: ____/ ____/ _____

Today, I am grateful for:

_____

_____

_____

How will I make today awesome?

_____

_____

_____

Positive affirmations:

_____

_____

_____

"The purpose of our lives is to be happy."
-- Dalai Lama

Today's amazing moments:

_____

_____

_____

How could I have made this day even better?

_____

_____

_____

Goals/Plans for Tomorrow: I am feeling:

_____   😊   😐   ☹️

_____

Date: ____/ ____/ _____

Today, I am grateful for:

_____

_____

_____

How will I make today awesome?

_____

_____

_____

Positive affirmations:

_____

_____

_____

"Change your thoughts and you change your world."
– Norman Vincent Peale

Today's amazing moments:

_____

_____

_____

How could I have made this day even better?

_____

_____

_____

Goals/Plans for Tomorrow: I am feeling:

_____   ☺ 😐 ☹

_____

Date: _____/ _____/ _____

Today, I am grateful for:

_____
_____
_____

How will I make today awesome?

_____
_____

Positive affirmations:

_____
_____
_____

"Well done is better than well said."
– Benjamin Franklin

Today's amazing moments:

_____
_____
_____

How could I have made this day even better?

_____
_____
_____

Goals/Plans for Tomorrow: I am feeling:

_____
_____   😊 😐 ☹️

Date: ____/ ____/ _____

Today, I am grateful for:

_____

_____

_____

How will I make today awesome?

_____

_____

_____

Positive affirmations:

_____

_____

_____

"Don't wait. The time will never be just right."
– Napoleon Hill

Today's amazing moments:

_____

_____

_____

How could I have made this day even better?

_____

_____

_____

Goals/Plans for Tomorrow: I am feeling:

_____

_____   ☺   😐   ☹

Date: _____ / _____ / _____

Today, I am grateful for:

_____

_____

_____

How will I make today awesome?

_____

_____

_____

Positive affirmations:

_____

_____

_____

"The best way out is always through."
-- Robert Frost

Today's amazing moments:

_____

_____

_____

How could I have made this day even better?

_____

_____

_____

Goals/Plans for Tomorrow: I am feeling:

_____

_____   😊 😐 ☹️

Monthly Reflection:

Looking back:

Wins:

_____

_____

_____

Distractions: Excuses:

_____   _____

_____   _____

_____   _____

"The aim of an argument or discussion
should not be victory, but progress."
– Joseph Joubert

Looking ahead:

Goals:

_____

_____

_____

Improvements:

_____

_____

_____

Notes:

_____

_____

_____

Date: _____ / _____ / _____

Today, I am grateful for:

_____

_____

_____

How will I make today awesome?

_____

_____

_____

Positive affirmations:

_____

_____

_____

"Do one thing each day that scares you."
– Eleanor Roosevelt

Today's amazing moments:

_____

_____

_____

How could I have made this day even better?

_____

_____

_____

Goals/Plans for Tomorrow: I am feeling:

_____

_____   ☺ 😐 ☹

Date: ____ / ____ / _____

Today, I am grateful for:

_____

_____

_____

How will I make today awesome?

_____

_____

_____

Positive affirmations:

_____

_____

_____

Success is the sum of small efforts,
repeated day in and day out.
— Robert Collier

Today's amazing moments:

_____

_____

_____

How could I have made this day even better?

_____

_____

_____

Goals/Plans for Tomorrow: I am feeling:

_____

_____   ☺ 😐 ☹

Today, I am grateful for:

How will I make today awesome?

Positive affirmations:

"You're only limit is you."
– Unknown

Today's amazing moments:

How could I have made this day even better?

Goals/Plans for Tomorrow: I am feeling:

Date: _____ / _____ / _____

Today, I am grateful for:

_____

_____

_____

How will I make today awesome?

_____

_____

Positive affirmations:

_____

_____

_____

"Wherever you are, be all there."
— Jim Elliot

Today's amazing moments:

_____

_____

_____

How could I have made this day even better?

_____

_____

_____

Goals/Plans for Tomorrow: I am feeling:

_____

_____   ☺ 😐 ☹

39

Date: _____/ _____/ _____

Today, I am grateful for:

_____

_____

_____

How will I make today awesome?

_____

_____

_____

Positive affirmations:

_____

_____

_____

*"Your imagination is your preview of
life's coming attractions."*
– Albert Einstein

Today's amazing moments:

_____

_____

_____

How could I have made this day even better?

_____

_____

_____

Goals/Plans for Tomorrow: I am feeling:

_____

_____   😊 😐 ☹️

Date: _____ / _____ / _____

Today, I am grateful for:

_____

_____

_____

How will I make today awesome?

_____

_____

_____

Positive affirmations:

_____

_____

_____

*"It often takes more courage to change
one's opinion than to keep it."*
— Willy Brandt

Today's amazing moments:

_____

_____

_____

How could I have made this day even better?

_____

_____

_____

Goals/Plans for Tomorrow: I am feeling:

_____   ☺ 😐 ☹

_____

Date: _____ / _____ / _____

Today, I am grateful for:

_____

_____

_____

How will I make today awesome?

_____

_____

_____

Positive affirmations:

_____

_____

_____

"Inspiration does exist, but it must find you working."
– Pablo Picasso

Today's amazing moments:

_____

_____

_____

How could I have made this day even better?

_____

_____

_____

Goals/Plans for Tomorrow: I am feeling:

_____

Date: ____/ ____/ _____

Today, I am grateful for:

_____

_____

_____

How will I make today awesome?

_____

_____

Positive affirmations:

_____

_____

_____

"If you try, you risk failure.
If you don't, you ensure it."
– Anonymous

Today's amazing moments:

_____

_____

_____

How could I have made this day even better?

_____

_____

_____

Goals/Plans for Tomorrow: I am feeling:

_____

_____   ☺ 😐 ☹

Date: ____ / ____ / _____

Today, I am grateful for:

_____

_____

_____

How will I make today awesome?

_____

_____

Positive affirmations:

_____

_____

_____

"Setting goals is the first step in turning
the invisible into the visible."
– Tony Robbins

Today's amazing moments:

_____

_____

_____

How could I have made this day even better?

_____

_____

_____

Goals/Plans for Tomorrow: I am feeling:

_____

Today, I am grateful for:

_____

_____

_____

How will I make today awesome?

_____

_____

_____

Positive affirmations:

_____

_____

_____

"The harder the conflict, the more glorious the triumph."
– Thomas Paine

Today's amazing moments:

_____

_____

_____

How could I have made this day even better?

_____

_____

_____

Goals/Plans for Tomorrow: I am feeling:

_____   ☺ 😐 ☹

Date: _____ / _____ / _____

Today, I am grateful for:

_____

_____

_____

How will I make today awesome?

_____

_____

Positive affirmations:

_____

_____

"Your attitude, not your aptitude,
will determine your altitude."
– Zig Ziglar

Today's amazing moments:

_____

_____

_____

How could I have made this day even better?

_____

_____

_____

Goals/Plans for Tomorrow: I am feeling:

_____

😊 😐 ☹️

Date: ____/ ____/ _____

Today, I am grateful for:

_____

_____

_____

How will I make today awesome?

_____

_____

_____

Positive affirmations:

_____

_____

_____

"What we dwell on is who we become."
– Oprah Winfrey

Today's amazing moments:

_____

_____

_____

How could I have made this day even better?

_____

_____

_____

Goals/Plans for Tomorrow: I am feeling:

_____

_____   ☺ 😐 ☹

Date: _____/ _____/ _____

Today, I am grateful for:

_____

_____

_____

How will I make today awesome?

_____

_____

Positive affirmations:

_____

_____

_____

"It is well to be up before daybreak, for such habits contribute to health, wealth, and wisdom."
– Aristotle

Today's amazing moments:

_____

_____

_____

How could I have made this day even better?

_____

_____

_____

Goals/Plans for Tomorrow: I am feeling:

_____   😊   😐   ☹️

_____

Date: ____ / ____ / _____

Today, I am grateful for:

_____
_____
_____

How will I make today awesome?

_____
_____
_____

Positive affirmations:

_____
_____
_____

*"You must not only aim right, but draw the bow
with all your might."*
– Henry David Thoreau

Today's amazing moments:

_____
_____
_____

How could I have made this day even better?

_____
_____
_____

Goals/Plans for Tomorrow: I am feeling:

_____   ☺   😐   ☹
_____

Date: _____/ _____/ _____

Today, I am grateful for:

_____

_____

_____

How will I make today awesome?

_____

_____

_____

Positive affirmations:

_____

_____

_____

*"Don't worry about failures, worry about
the chances you miss when you don't even try."*
– Jack Canfield

Today's amazing moments:

_____

_____

_____

How could I have made this day even better?

_____

_____

_____

Goals/Plans for Tomorrow: I am feeling:

_____

_____   ☺ 😐 ☹

Date: ____/ ____/ _____

Today, I am grateful for:

_____

_____

_____

How will I make today awesome?

_____

_____

Positive affirmations:

_____

_____

_____

"Though no one can go back and make a brand new start,
anyone can start from now and make a brand new ending."
– Carl Bard

Today's amazing moments:

_____

_____

_____

How could I have made this day even better?

_____

_____

_____

Goals/Plans for Tomorrow: I am feeling:

_____   😊 😐 🙁

_____

Date: _____ / _____ / _____

Today, I am grateful for:

_____

_____

_____

How will I make today awesome?

_____

_____

_____

Positive affirmations:

_____

_____

_____

"An obstacle is often a stepping stone."
– William Prescott

Today's amazing moments:

_____

_____

_____

How could I have made this day even better?

_____

_____

_____

Goals/Plans for Tomorrow: I am feeling:

_____

_____   ☺ 😐 ☹

Date: ____/ ____/ _____

Today, I am grateful for:

_____

_____

_____

How will I make today awesome?

_____

_____

_____

Positive affirmations:

_____

_____

_____

*"Never give up on something that you can't go
a day without thinking about."*
– Unknown

Today's amazing moments:

_____

_____

_____

How could I have made this day even better?

_____

_____

_____

Goals/Plans for Tomorrow: I am feeling:

_____

😊 😐 ☹️

Date: _____ / _____ / _____

Today, I am grateful for:

_____

_____

_____

How will I make today awesome?

_____

_____

_____

Positive affirmations:

_____

_____

_____

*"Keep your face to the sunshine
and you can never see the shadow."*
– Helen Keller

Today's amazing moments:

_____

_____

_____

How could I have made this day even better?

_____

_____

_____

Goals/Plans for Tomorrow: I am feeling:

_____

_____   😊   😐   🙁

Date: ____/ ____/ _____

Today, I am grateful for:

_____

_____

_____

How will I make today awesome?

_____

_____

Positive affirmations:

_____

_____

_____

"When you arise in the morning, think of what a precious privilege
it is to be alive – to breathe, to think, to enjoy, to love."
– Marcus Aurelius

Today's amazing moments:

_____

_____

_____

How could I have made this day even better?

_____

_____

_____

Goals/Plans for Tomorrow: I am feeling:

_____   😊   😐   ☹️

Date: _____/ _____/ _____

Today, I am grateful for:

_____

_____

_____

How will I make today awesome?

_____

_____

_____

Positive affirmations:

_____

_____

_____

"Every day may not be good,
but there's something good in every day."
– Alice Morse Earle

Today's amazing moments:

_____

_____

_____

How could I have made this day even better?

_____

_____

_____

Goals/Plans for Tomorrow: I am feeling:

_____

_____   ☺ 😐 ☹

Date: ____/ ____/ _____

Today, I am grateful for:

_____

_____

_____

How will I make today awesome?

_____

_____

Positive affirmations:

_____

_____

_____

*"It's not about having the right opportunities.
It's about handling the opportunities right."*
– Mark Hunter

Today's amazing moments:

_____

_____

_____

How could I have made this day even better?

_____

_____

_____

Goals/Plans for Tomorrow: I am feeling:

_____   😊 😐 🙁

Date: ____/ ____/ _____

Today, I am grateful for:

_____

_____

_____

How will I make today awesome?

_____

_____

Positive affirmations:

_____

_____

_____

"Happiness is not something readymade.
It comes from your own actions." – Dalai Lama

Today's amazing moments:

_____

_____

_____

How could I have made this day even better?

_____

_____

_____

Goals/Plans for Tomorrow: I am feeling:

_____

_____   ☺ 😐 ☹

Date: _____ / _____ / _____

Today, I am grateful for:

_____

_____

_____

How will I make today awesome?

_____

_____

Positive affirmations:

_____

_____

_____

"What you do speaks so loudly that I cannot hear what you say."
– Ralph Waldo Emerson

Today's amazing moments:

_____

_____

_____

How could I have made this day even better?

_____

_____

_____

Goals/Plans for Tomorrow: I am feeling:

_____

Date: _____/ _____/ _____

Today, I am grateful for:

_____

_____

_____

How will I make today awesome?

_____

_____

_____

Positive affirmations:

_____

_____

_____

"Tough times never last, but tough people do."
– Dr. Robert Schuller

Today's amazing moments:

_____

_____

_____

How could I have made this day even better?

_____

_____

_____

Goals/Plans for Tomorrow: I am feeling:

_____

_____   ☺   😐   ☹

Today, I am grateful for:

_____

_____

_____

How will I make today awesome?

_____

_____

Positive affirmations:

_____

_____

_____

*""I simply wake up every morning a better person
than when I went to bed."
– Sidney Poitier*

Today's amazing moments:

_____

_____

_____

How could I have made this day even better?

_____

_____

_____

Goals/Plans for Tomorrow: I am feeling:

_____   ☺ 😐 ☹

Today, I am grateful for:

_____

_____

_____

How will I make today awesome?

_____

_____

_____

Positive affirmations:

_____

_____

_____

"I'm going to make everything around me beautiful
– that will be my life."
– Elsie De Wolfe

Today's amazing moments:

_____

_____

_____

How could I have made this day even better?

_____

_____

_____

Goals/Plans for Tomorrow: I am feeling:

_____

_____   😊 😐 🙁

Date: _____/ _____/ _____

Today, I am grateful for:

_____

_____

_____

How will I make today awesome?

_____

_____

_____

Positive affirmations:

_____

_____

_____

"All our dreams can come true –
if we have the courage to pursue them."
– Walt Disney

Today's amazing moments:

_____

_____

_____

How could I have made this day even better?

_____

_____

_____

Goals/Plans for Tomorrow: I am feeling:

_____   😊 😐 ☹️

Date: _____ / _____ / _____

Today, I am grateful for:

_____

_____

_____

How will I make today awesome?

_____

_____

_____

Positive affirmations:

_____

_____

_____

"The best way to predict the future is to invent it."
– Alan Kay

Today's amazing moments:

_____

_____

_____

How could I have made this day even better?

_____

_____

_____

Goals/Plans for Tomorrow: I am feeling:

_____

_____   ☺ 😐 ☹

Monthly Reflection:

Date: ____/ ____/ _____

Looking back:

Wins:

_____

_____

_____

Distractions: Excuses:

_____   _____

_____   _____

_____   _____

The future depends on what you do today.
— Mahatma Gandhi

Looking ahead:

Goals:

_____

_____

_____

Improvements:

_____

_____

_____

Notes:

_____

_____

_____

Date: ____/ ____/ _____

Today, I am grateful for:

_____

_____

_____

How will I make today awesome?

_____

_____

_____

Positive affirmations:

_____

_____

_____

"Every strike brings me closer to the next home run."
– Babe Ruth

Today's amazing moments:

_____

_____

_____

How could I have made this day even better?

_____

_____

_____

Goals/Plans for Tomorrow: I am feeling:

_____

_____   ☺ ☺ ☹

Date: ____/ ____/ _____

Today, I am grateful for:

_____

_____

_____

How will I make today awesome?

_____

_____

_____

Positive affirmations:

_____

_____

_____

"Treat objections as requests for further information."
-- Brian Tracy

Today's amazing moments:

_____

_____

_____

How could I have made this day even better?

_____

_____

_____

Goals/Plans for Tomorrow: I am feeling:

_____   ☺ 😐 ☹

Date: ____/ ____/ _____

Today, I am grateful for:

_____

_____

_____

How will I make today awesome?

_____

_____

_____

Positive affirmations:

_____

_____

_____

"Courage is never to let your actions be influenced by your fears."
– Arthur Koestler

Today's amazing moments:

_____

_____

_____

How could I have made this day even better?

_____

_____

_____

Goals/Plans for Tomorrow: I am feeling:

_____   :) :| :(

_____

Date: _____/ _____/ _____

Today, I am grateful for:

_____
_____
_____

How will I make today awesome?

_____
_____
_____

Positive affirmations:

_____
_____
_____

"The only thing in your control is effort.
That's all, and that's everything."
– Mark Cuban

Today's amazing moments:

_____
_____
_____

How could I have made this day even better?

_____
_____
_____

Goals/Plans for Tomorrow: I am feeling:

_____   😊   😐   🙁
_____

Date: ____/ ____/ _____

Today, I am grateful for:

_____

_____

_____

How will I make today awesome?

_____

_____

_____

Positive affirmations:

_____

_____

_____

"Whether you think you can or you can't, you're right."
– Henry Ford

Today's amazing moments:

_____

_____

_____

How could I have made this day even better?

_____

_____

_____

Goals/Plans for Tomorrow: I am feeling:

_____   😊   😐   🙁

_____

70

Today, I am grateful for:

_____

_____

_____

How will I make today awesome?

_____

_____

_____

Positive affirmations:

_____

_____

_____

"When at a conflict between mind and heart,
always follow your heart."
– Swami Vivekananda

Today's amazing moments:

_____

_____

_____

How could I have made this day even better?

_____

_____

_____

Goals/Plans for Tomorrow: I am feeling:

_____   😊 😐 ☹️

Date: ____ / ____ / _____

Today, I am grateful for:

How will I make today awesome?

Positive affirmations:

"Don't judge each day by the harvest you reap
but by the seeds that you plant."
– Robert Louis Stevenson

Today's amazing moments:

How could I have made this day even better?

Goals/Plans for Tomorrow: I am feeling:

Date: ____/ ____/ _____

Today, I am grateful for:

_____

_____

_____

How will I make today awesome?

_____

_____

_____

Positive affirmations:

_____

_____

_____

"To live is the rarest thing in the world.
Most people exist, that is all."
– Oscar Wilde

Today's amazing moments:

_____

_____

_____

How could I have made this day even better?

_____

_____

_____

Goals/Plans for Tomorrow: I am feeling:

_____

_____

Date: ____/ ____/ _____

Today, I am grateful for:

_____

_____

_____

How will I make today awesome?

_____

_____

_____

Positive affirmations:

_____

_____

_____

"Only those who will risk going too far
can possibly find out how far one can go."
– T.S. Eliot

Today's amazing moments:

_____

_____

_____

How could I have made this day even better?

_____

_____

_____

Goals/Plans for Tomorrow: I am feeling:

_____

_____   ☺ 😐 ☹

Date: ____ / ____ / _____

Today, I am grateful for:

_____

_____

_____

How will I make today awesome?

_____

_____

_____

Positive affirmations:

_____

_____

_____

"Just keep going. Everybody gets better if they keep at it."
– Ted Williams

Today's amazing moments:

_____

_____

_____

How could I have made this day even better?

_____

_____

_____

Goals/Plans for Tomorrow: I am feeling:

_____

Today, I am grateful for:

_____

_____

_____

How will I make today awesome?

_____

_____

Positive affirmations:

_____

_____

"It is never too late to be what you might have been."
– George Eliot

Today's amazing moments:

_____

_____

_____

How could I have made this day even better?

_____

_____

_____

Goals/Plans for Tomorrow: I am feeling:

_____

_____   😊   😐   🙁

Today, I am grateful for:

_____

_____

_____

How will I make today awesome?

_____

_____

_____

Positive affirmations:

_____

_____

_____

"Don't wish it were easier, wish you were better."
– Jim Rohn

Today's amazing moments:

_____

_____

_____

How could I have made this day even better?

_____

_____

_____

Goals/Plans for Tomorrow: I am feeling:

_____

_____   😊 😐 ☹️

Date: ____/ ____/ _____

Today, I am grateful for:

_____

_____

_____

How will I make today awesome?

_____

_____

_____

Positive affirmations:

_____

_____

_____

"Never let your memories be greater than your dreams."
– Doug Ivester

Today's amazing moments:

_____

_____

_____

How could I have made this day even better?

_____

_____

_____

Goals/Plans for Tomorrow: I am feeling:

_____

_____   😊 😐 ☹️

Date: ____ / ____ / _____

Today, I am grateful for:

_____

_____

_____

How will I make today awesome?

_____

_____

_____

Positive affirmations:

_____

_____

_____

"Nothing important was ever achieved
without someone taking a chance."
– H. Jackson Brown, Jr

Today's amazing moments:

_____

_____

_____

How could I have made this day even better?

_____

_____

_____

Goals/Plans for Tomorrow: I am feeling:

_____   ☺ 😐 ☹

Date: ____/ ____/ _____

Today, I am grateful for:

_____

_____

_____

How will I make today awesome?

_____

_____

_____

Positive affirmations:

_____

_____

_____

"There are two primary choices in life: to accept conditions as they exist, or accept the responsibility for changing them."
– Denis Waitley

Today's amazing moments:

_____

_____

_____

How could I have made this day even better?

_____

_____

_____

Goals/Plans for Tomorrow: I am feeling:

_____

_____   :) :| :(

Date: ____/ ____/ _____

Today, I am grateful for:

_____

_____

_____

How will I make today awesome?

_____

_____

_____

Positive affirmations:

_____

_____

*"In three words I can sum up everything
I've learned about life: It goes on."
– Robert Frost*

Today's amazing moments:

_____

_____

_____

How could I have made this day even better?

_____

_____

_____

Goals/Plans for Tomorrow: I am feeling:

_____

_____   😊   😐   🙁

Date: ____/ ____/ _____

Today, I am grateful for:

_____

_____

_____

How will I make today awesome?

_____

_____

_____

Positive affirmations:

_____

_____

_____

"If you aim at nothing, you will hit it every time."
– Zig Ziglar

Today's amazing moments:

_____

_____

_____

How could I have made this day even better?

_____

_____

_____

Goals/Plans for Tomorrow: I am feeling:

_____

_____   ☺ ☺ ☹

Today, I am grateful for:

_____

_____

_____

How will I make today awesome?

_____

_____

Positive affirmations:

_____

_____

_____

"If you're offered a seat on a rocket ship,
don't ask what seat! Just get on."
– Sheryl Sandberg

Today's amazing moments:

_____

_____

_____

How could I have made this day even better?

_____

_____

_____

Goals/Plans for Tomorrow: I am feeling:

_____

Date: ____ / ____ / _____

Today, I am grateful for:

_____

_____

_____

How will I make today awesome?

_____

_____

_____

Positive affirmations:

_____

_____

_____

"People often say that motivation doesn't last.
Well, neither does bathing. That's why we recommend it daily."
– Zig Ziglar

Today's amazing moments:

_____

_____

_____

How could I have made this day even better?

_____

_____

_____

Goals/Plans for Tomorrow: I am feeling:

_____   ☺ 😐 ☹

_____

Date: ____/ ____/ _____

Today, I am grateful for:

_____

_____

_____

How will I make today awesome?

_____

_____

_____

Positive affirmations:

_____

_____

_____

"The creation of a thousand forests is in one acorn."
– Ralph Waldo Emerson

Today's amazing moments:

_____

_____

_____

How could I have made this day even better?

_____

_____

_____

Goals/Plans for Tomorrow: I am feeling:

_____   ☺ 😐 ☹

Date: _____ / _____ / _____

Today, I am grateful for:

_____

_____

_____

How will I make today awesome?

_____

_____

Positive affirmations:

_____

_____

_____

"Always be a first-rate version of yourself,
instead of a second-rate version of somebody else."
– Judy Garland

Today's amazing moments:

_____

_____

_____

How could I have made this day even better?

_____

_____

_____

Goals/Plans for Tomorrow: I am feeling:

_____   ☺ 😐 ☹

_____

Date: ____/ ____/ _____

Today, I am grateful for:

_____

_____

_____

How will I make today awesome?

_____

_____

_____

Positive affirmations:

_____

_____

_____

"Smile in the mirror. Do that every morning and
you'll start to see a big difference in your life."
– Yoko Ono

Today's amazing moments:

_____

_____

_____

How could I have made this day even better?

_____

_____

_____

Goals/Plans for Tomorrow: I am feeling:

_____

_____

Date: ____ / ____ / _____

Today, I am grateful for:

_____

_____

_____

How will I make today awesome?

_____

_____

Positive affirmations:

_____

_____

"I am not a product of my circumstances.
I am a product of my decisions."
– Stephen Covey

Today's amazing moments:

_____

_____

_____

How could I have made this day even better?

_____

_____

_____

Goals/Plans for Tomorrow: I am feeling:

_____   😊 😐 🙁

Date: _____ / _____ / _____

Today, I am grateful for:

_____

_____

_____

How will I make today awesome?

_____

_____

Positive affirmations:

_____

_____

_____

"Challenge yourself with something you know you could never do,
and what you'll find is that you can overcome anything."
– Unknown

Today's amazing moments:

_____

_____

_____

How could I have made this day even better?

_____

_____

_____

Goals/Plans for Tomorrow: I am feeling:

_____

_____   😊   😐   ☹️

Date: _____/ _____/ _____

Today, I am grateful for:

_____
_____
_____

How will I make today awesome?

_____
_____
_____

Positive affirmations:

_____
_____
_____

"Minds are like parachutes – they only function when open."
– Thomas Dewar

Today's amazing moments:

_____
_____
_____

How could I have made this day even better?

_____
_____
_____

Goals/Plans for Tomorrow: I am feeling:

_____
_____   😊   😐   ☹️

Date: ____ / ____ / _____

Today, I am grateful for:

_____

_____

_____

How will I make today awesome?

_____

_____

_____

Positive affirmations:

_____

_____

_____

"The best way to have a good idea is to have lots of ideas."
– Linus Pauling

Today's amazing moments:

_____

_____

_____

How could I have made this day even better?

_____

_____

_____

Goals/Plans for Tomorrow: I am feeling:

_____   ☺ 😐 ☹

Date: _____/ _____/ _____

Today, I am grateful for:

_____

_____

_____

How will I make today awesome?

_____

_____

_____

Positive affirmations:

_____

_____

_____

"Creativity is the power to connect the seemingly unconnected."
– William Plomer

Today's amazing moments:

_____

_____

_____

How could I have made this day even better?

_____

_____

_____

Goals/Plans for Tomorrow: I am feeling:

_____

_____   😊 😐 ☹️

Date: _____ / _____ / _____

Today, I am grateful for:

_____

_____

_____

How will I make today awesome?

_____

_____

_____

Positive affirmations:

_____

_____

_____

"If opportunity doesn't knock, build a door."
– Milton Berle

Today's amazing moments:

_____

_____

_____

How could I have made this day even better?

_____

_____

_____

Goals/Plans for Tomorrow: I am feeling:

_____   😊   😐   ☹️

Date: ____/ ____/ _____

Today, I am grateful for:

_____

_____

_____

How will I make today awesome?

_____

_____

_____

Positive affirmations:

_____

_____

_____

"We cannot change the cards we are dealt,
just how we play the hand."
– Randy Pausch

Today's amazing moments:

_____

_____

_____

How could I have made this day even better?

_____

_____

_____

Goals/Plans for Tomorrow: I am feeling:

_____

😊   😐   🙁

94

Today, I am grateful for:

_____

_____

_____

How will I make today awesome?

_____

_____

Positive affirmations:

_____

_____

_____

It is not in the stars to hold our destiny, but in ourselves."
– William Shakespeare

Today's amazing moments:

_____

_____

_____

How could I have made this day even better?

_____

_____

_____

Goals/Plans for Tomorrow: I am feeling:

_____   😊 😐 🙁

Date: _____ / _____ / _____

Today, I am grateful for:

_____
_____
_____

How will I make today awesome?

_____
_____
_____

Positive affirmations:

_____
_____
_____

"If you cannot do great things, do small things in a great way."
– Napoleon Hill

Today's amazing moments:

_____
_____
_____

How could I have made this day even better?

_____
_____
_____

Goals/Plans for Tomorrow: I am feeling:

_____
_____   😊 😐 ☹️

Monthly Reflection:

Date: _____/ _____/ _____

Looking back:

Wins:

_____

_____

_____

Distractions: Excuses:

_____   _____

_____   _____

_____   _____

"What lies behind us and what lies before us
are tiny matters compared to what lies within us."
– Henry S. Haskins

Looking ahead:

Goals:

_____

_____

_____

Improvements:

_____

_____

_____

Notes:

_____

_____

Share the joy with kids!
Help them cultivate the attitude of gratitude:

ISBN: 1696006740

Hi!

My name is Sujatha Lalgudi.
Thank you for purchasing this book.

I hope you found this journal to be helpful in your journey of gratitude and happiness and will continue the practice...

Write to me at sujatha.lalgudi@gmail.com with the subject as **Gratitude** to get free printable coloring pages to practice mindfulness & relaxation.

If you liked this book, please leave me a review on Amazon! Your kind reviews and comments will encourage me to make more books like this.

Thank you
Sujatha Lalgudi

Be Thankful!

Celebrate your Success!

Share the Joy!

Feel Great Everyday!